This journal is given to

____

on ____________________________

from __________________________

Grandmother's Story

Your birth date and place of birth:

Your parents' names:

Your brothers and sisters, from oldest to youngest:

Names of other close family members:

Date and place you married Grandpa:

Grandpa's parents' names:

His brothers and sisters, from oldest to youngest:

Mom/Dad's birth date and place of birth:

My aunts and uncles, from oldest to youngest:

Our Family History

Where is your side of the family from originally?

How did they get to this country?

What did they do for work once they came here?

Where is Grandpa’s family from originally?

What are some stories your parents shared with you about their childhoods?

Tell me about some of the more interesting members of our family.

What are some of the biggest challenges or setbacks our family has faced? How did we get through them?

What are some of the happiest times our family has experienced?

What is something I may not know about our family?

Every family has a few skeletons in the closet.
What are some of ours?

What physical family traits do I seem to have?

What personality traits have I inherited?

Whom do I most remind you of in our family?

What were you like as a child?

What special interests did you have when you were a child?

Early Years

What story is most often told about your early years?

Who were you told you looked like and why?

Where did you live when you were a child?

What did your parents do for a living?

What kinds of values did your parents instill in you as a child?

How do you think these values helped you later in life?

Did you have a nickname growing up?
If so, who gave it to you and why?

What were some of your favorite animals as a child?

Did you have any interesting encounters with animals?

Who were your best friends when you were little?

What were they like?

Did you have any pets growing up? Tell me about them.

What types of games did you like to play?

What were your favorite toys? Why did you love them so?

What were your favorite books?

What were your favorite songs?

Did any inventions change your family's life?

What are some modern inventions that you never would have dreamed of back then?

What are some benefits to slower-moving times that you wish I could experience?

What did your family do in the evenings for entertainment?

What was a hard lesson you had to learn?

Your Parents and Grandparents

What is your most cherished memory of your mother?

What were some of your mother's sayings?

Describe your mother's sense of humor.

What is your most cherished memory of your father?

What were some of your father's sayings?

Describe your father's sense of humor.

What is your most cherished memory of your grandmother?

What were some of your grandmother's sayings?

Describe your grandmother's sense of humor.

What is your most cherished memory of your grandfather?

What were some of your grandfather's sayings?

Describe your grandfather's sense of humor.

School Days

What did you want to be when you grew up?

Who were your heroes and why?

Did the family have any special heroes?

What were your favorite subjects in school?

Did you have any favorite teachers? What was so special about them?

What did you dislike about school?

Did you belong to any clubs in school?

On an average day, what did you do after school?

What were some of your favorite movies?

Did you have favorite actors/actresses?

Did you remind people of someone famous?

What did you worry about most as a teenager?

How did you spend your summers?

Did your family take vacations?

What were some of your favorite vacation destinations?

Describe a fun night out when you were a teenager.

Who was your very first date? Where did he take you?

When You Met Grandpa

When did you meet Grandpa?

What were your first impressions of him?

If someone had told you early on that you were going to marry Grandpa, what would you have said?

Where did you and Grandpa go for your first date?
How was it?

What did your parents think of Grandpa?

How did Grandpa pop the question?

Tell me about your wedding ceremony. Who was in the wedding party?

What were some of the most memorable moments of your wedding day?

After the ceremony, how did you celebrate?

Did you go on a honeymoon? If so, where?

Where did you live as newlyweds?

Did you work? If so, what did your job entail?

How did you celebrate your first anniversary?

What have you learned about marriage and relationships that you would use to give advice to young couples?

What was an aspect of marriage that you didn't expect?

Tell me about the favorite place you lived in.

What interesting other places have you lived in?

Children

How did you tell Grandpa you were pregnant with Mom/Dad?

How did Grandpa react to the happy news?

What was the best part about being pregnant with Mom/Dad?

How did you choose a name for Mom/Dad?

Did the name have any special significance?

What other names did you consider?

Did you have any jobs while you were raising your children? What were they?

How did having a child change your life?

Did you have any time to yourself during those years?
What activities or hobbies did you pursue?

What did you find most challenging about parenthood?

What did you find most rewarding about parenthood?

Who did Mom/Dad look like when she/he was a baby?

What were Mom's/Dad's first words?

Tell me about some other firsts.

What were Mom's/Dad's favorite childhood toys?

What were some favorite stories and songs?

What is your favorite embarrassing story about Mom/Dad?

What is a story people like to tell about you?

What were some hard lessons you learned as a parent?

Tell me about my aunts/uncles. Did Mom/Dad get along with his/her siblings?

What career path did you think Mom/Dad would pursue when she/he grew up?

As a child, how did Mom/Dad most often get into trouble?

What was Mom/Dad like when she/he was a teenager?

Tell me about a time when Mom/Dad made you proud.

When did my parents meet?

What did you think when my parents first announced they were getting married?

What was the most memorable part of their wedding ceremony?

What was the most memorable part of their wedding reception?

You and Me

What was your reaction when you heard I was on the way?

Did you give my mother any particular advice?

What sort of general parenting advice did you give to my mom and dad?

Describe the first time you saw me. How did you feel?

Whom do you think I most resembled as a baby?

What kinds of things did we do together when I was a little older?

What did I show an early preference for?

Did I have any strong likes or dislikes?

What career paths did you see in my future?

Did I have a favorite pretend activity?

What is your favorite memory of me as a child?

What is your favorite family holiday and why?

Tell me about a favorite holiday tradition in our family.

What holiday tradition would you like to see me continue?

Tell me about a time when you have been particularly proud of me.

Share a favorite dinner recipe...

Share a favorite dessert recipe...

Share a favorite holiday recipe...

What is your best trick for fixing a bad day?

Who in the family are you most similar to?

Do you see similarities between us when you were my age?

In what ways are we different?

How am I like my parents?

What most surprises you about your grandchildren?

What do you say when people ask about me?

What is one of your favorite ways to spend time with me?

What is an unexpected perk of being a grandma?

Looking Forward

Is there anything you want me to enjoy or try in the future?

What is your most treasured possession?

Is there an heirloom you wish to be remembered by?

Is there any jewelry that has special significance to you?

Are there any hobbies you still want to try?

Are there important life tasks you still want to complete?

Are there places you still want to visit?

What do you think is the most important lesson you have taught me?

What do you think is the most important lesson I have taught you?

What would you change if you had to do it all over again?

What is the best piece of advice you ever received?

What is one thing you hope I will remember in difficult times?

If you could share one key piece of advice about love and marriage, what would it be?

If you could share one key piece of advice about money and finances, what would it be?

If you could share one key piece of advice about parenting, what would it be?

Looking back on your life, what accomplishments are you most proud of?

What is one thing that you always want me to remember about you?

More Stories...